A New Way of Being: How to Rewire Your Brain and Take Control of Your Life

Dan Desmarques

Published by 22 Lions Bookstore, 2019.

Copyright Page

A New Way of Being: How to Rewire Your Brain and Take Control of Your Life

By Dan Desmarques

Copyright © Dan Desmarques, 2019 (1st Ed.). All Rights Reserved..

Published by 22 Lions Bookstore and Publishing House

About the Publisher

About the 22 Lions Bookstore:

www.22Lions.com

Facebook.com/22Lions

Twitter.com/22lionsbookshop

Instagram.com/22lionsbookshop

Pinterest.com/22lionsbookshop

Introduction

The consciousness of the soul manifests itself in several planes of reality interconnected with each other. In all these planes, there is the permanence of the unique spirit of the being. Therefore, the spirit can manifest itself in different space-time constructs. This explains why it is possible to perform astral travels to other planets or to make quantum leaps to parallel realities. On the other hand, whenever the soul incarnates in a certain plane of reality, as for example, the planet earth, it can incarnate in different periods of history, without there being a temporal obligatory cycle as we know it. Thus, a human being of the future can easily reincarnate in any past period of time and vice versa. This is why time is not only an illusion, scientifically verifiable, but also a necessary illusion, like so many others.

Along this line of perceptions, we must know and explore all these dynamics with a pragmatic perspective, and we begin this by asking: "who are we and why do we live?" These questions, among many others, are clarified here, leading to a better understanding of the mechanism of life. In fact, "all truths are easy to understand as soon as they are discovered; the difficulty is to discover them "(Galileo Galilei). Throughout the several chapters, a linear spiritual approach is presented, cross-referenced with different religious, as well as gnostic, perspectives, while focusing on empirical premises. In this way, the idea of knowing how to live without the fear of chaos is promoted, allowing learnings which lead to greater happiness and success in life.

Who Are We?

A human being is composed of the same elements that form the universe. This is because he is himself a synthesis of the universe itself. And yet he and his body are not the same, for the spirit, which forms, or must form the most prominent part of the personality, contains the divine spark, a small portion of the divine fire, made up of the very nature of God. And in this sense, it is wrong to say that we are God, but it is not wrong to say that we can be like a god, in the sense that, awareness brings the mind of man closer to the mind of God.

The state of Buddhahood or enlightenment is thus non-exclusive, but open and progressive, to all who desire such an approach, through meditation, knowledge and physical experience. And it is not possible without a formidable balance in these three planes. Any imbalance in one of these elements before the others, delays the progress of the individual in this walk.

On the other hand, to the extent that man possesses the same chemical elements that make up matter, he holds real power over the energy that moves matter and is itself a form of energy endowed with intelligence and controlled by the divine magnitude which guides the whole universe and the matter that it includes. In other words, although subject to the laws of time, a human being can actually manifest whatever reality he intends to live if he really knows how to control the mental laws governing that possibility. For such, he has to be able to control, discipline and persist in all the elements that make up his identity, namely his thoughts, his emotions, his actions, and all the other elements that interfere with them, including the thoughts of others, their emotions, and their actions.

Although telepathy is still a strange phenomenon to many, what we want others to think about us can actually be verbalized, thought-out and triggered through the communication we have with them, and the emotions we convey at any moment to such people. Communication is a much more complex medium than many may think, and it acquires deep genetic proportions that should not be ignored. For if, on the one hand, most of what we think corresponds to survival needs, on the other hand, it interferes with new social models that sometimes conflict with these values, and with our personal values.

If ever, when participating in an event, or interacting with a certain group of strangers, you felt an immediate repulsion or approach towards certain individuals, or cultures, you know that this emotion was later justified by the words and actions of such people. And we can actually create theories about the past, but such theories hardly cover all the causes behind our more emotional experiences.

Some call intuition to such abilities, but they actually include many more aspects of our being, and not simply intuition. Telepathy and the heart are closely related to thought, education, culture, and identity, as well as the relative importance we place on each of these elements.

As far as communication itself is concerned, by word or writing, although we cannot totally control how what we say affects others, we can, substantially, adapt to their responses, as well as communicate according to aspects that are more favorable to others. To do this, however, we need to identify relevant values. After all, all communication conveys personal values, and it is through these that we transform the world in which we live.

It is ridiculous to think that a person cannot change the world, because each person has contact with at least one hundred people, through the social means at his disposal, mainly with the Internet, and this number multiplies substantially, making a phrase or a photo able to achieve repercussions far beyond what would be expected.

With regard to gestures, in general, we tend to be more affable with people who touch or touch us. Hence the negative response we get when we touch someone who feels they are not yet at that level of affinity. And yet, this level can be created by touching, whether or not it exists between two or more people. This factor is so relevant that a simple hug can stimulate sexual desires in both men and women.

However, there are genetic factors behind how we react to touch. And much of these factors are related to physical attraction or signs of kindness. It is therefore not surprising that so many men in the world today are being grouped on a large scale into extinction, while a few others are chosen by women in general, who compete aggressively for them, for procreation, or at least casual sex that can lead to it, even though much of the female behavior is unconscious.

Communication, in its technical aspect, can never be relevant or sufficiently true without encompassing all the aspects mentioned.

How Do We Find Our Real Identity?

A human being is simultaneously the whole and the part, and also simultaneously the nothingness. God is in him and in the whole physical universe. And a human being can therefore communicate with the whole physical universe and with God, first, through a feeling of empathy and humility that eliminates the interference of the ego, and then behind a symbiosis of emotions and thoughts. This ability enables us not only to understand communications from God, but also the intentions of other human beings, and even animals.

Being composed of all elements interacting in the universe, the human being is the whole, since the whole resides in him; Being an element of this same universe, he is a part of the whole; But, being no more than an element ordered by the law of the divine, he is nothing in himself. And in this sense, personality exists and does not exist at the same time. Personality is a necessary illusion, which transforms and dissipates in time, and between lives, through the experiences, knowledge and achievements acquired. The more we learn and the more able we become, the less egocentric we are. And in this sense, we can say that art, as a path to complexity and the manifestation of harmony through chaos, represents the fastest path to spiritual ascension.

Despite the fact that originality is an illusion, realism is not. The identity of a being is manifest and exists because it cooperates with the sacred geometry of the universe, for only by being an element of the whole can the individual be as important as this whole. And so, a person is as important as he can disregard his importance, something that is only possible through ambition, the need for success, in all areas that are relevant to this same individual, from which stand the ability to love and to procreate through sex, the capacity to feel personal satisfaction and fulfillment through community service, understood by many as a job, although this is a very basic and unconscious stage of such manifestation, and finally, the capacity to be respected, which is misinterpreted by many as the ability to bully and gain value for nothing but existence itself.

True respect exists only when a human being respects himself, and this is only possible through integrity, understanding of social morality, in its essential defects and foundations, and the constant application of ethical acts.

The ego is a necessary illusion that leads to both arrogance and ignorance, because the realization of being something only obtains validity from divine or social presuppositions, and does not develop independently of either of these two perspectives. However, we say that the ego is a necessary illusion, because without it, it would not be possible to become aware of ignorance and arrogance, manifestations which only become negative when ignored and invisible.

It is said that a human being is blind and stupid, when he cannot see the arrogance of others and his own. And in this sense, idiots will always have power over other idiots. Such is the law of the universe, which unites compatible energies in order to exterminate the useless.

Although an individual is as important as the universe, as much as the energy he can control to create in that same universe, he is less important than an ant because he is subjugated to the laws of chance that govern his life and fears what others may think of his actions.

The relativity of this power can be positioned in levels of influence, which can be divided primarily into positive and negative, but must later be understood as primarily effective. For the being that has reached consciousness no longer thinks of right and wrong, truth or lie, positive or negative, but only purpose.

This noble purpose is so selfless that it is often confused by the masses with its opposite, psychosis, or self-destruction. This is because they both look the same to the ignorant masses — selfishness, madness and cruelty.

The artist who is in love with his work is very different from the junkie who paints graffitis in a street or on the wall of his apartment, and yet, for the social mass, composed mainly of imbeciles, they seem the same.

These are very different from each other. First, because the egoism of the artist is not really selfishness but altruism, extreme spirituality, in which only the artist and the creator participate in a work with a world impact, and the masses are being excluded from such participation precisely because they do not have the level necessary to be considered. Although many can enjoy a song, it does not mean that they can play the guitar they listen to or compose at the same level of the musical production.

As far as madness is concerned, it is a historical fact that the ignorant of this world have always considered crazy what they do not understand, although they hypocritically enjoy the goods created by those whom they called mad, namely the lamp, the car and the airplane, among others.

Cruelty is usually misunderstood by all who consider themselves good people. And most people believe they are good people. And yet, criticism of the imbecile is not an act of negativity or cruelty, but justice. The confusion arises from a child mentality present in the majority, which leads them to believe that if they are not in a prison or a psychiatric hospital, they are automatically endowed with the capacity to exist. This is not so. And insulting the imbecile is always a fair insult.

How to Eliminate the Negativity Within Us?

All kind of social influence is negative, for positive influence merely corresponds to the spheres of thought and spiritual dimension of individual consciousness. In this sense we can say that all who are immersed in the pleasure of the flesh are negative people by nature. For the pleasure of the flesh one understands not only sex, but also the pleasure of eating for pleasure instead of more health, the pleasure of killing, the pleasure of seeing others suffer, the pleasure of causing emotional or physical pain, and the pleasure of feeling superior to other beings, human or not.

All sorts of physical pleasure binds the human being to the negativity of the planet, the material negativity that eliminates it progressively. And it is a fact, that negative people, tend to die faster, and if that does not happen, to suffer for long periods of time, with physical pains, illnesses and even nightmares and insomnia. These are those who suffer most from the uncertainties of life, and also those who believe more in luck, because they do not understand the relation between their acts and the consequences of the same, do not understand the spiritual and energetic laws of the universe that they inhabit.

In this sense, a highly spiritual and positive being is one who, conscious of the consequences of his actions and in total absence of egocentrism, manifests a determining influence in his words and actions, even if endowed with a truth that can pierce, like a swords , all who listen to him. Here we find musicians, sculptors, writers and mystics, who live from divine power, feed on this energy, and despise the value of social opinion, whatever it may be. This is because the purpose of these, when conscious, pierces the fears and thoughts of the masses, not only of their time, but many more generations to come. These beings are unalterable in the face of any external changes, such as a boat sailing through storms. And we can therefore say that the power of a human being assumes himself in proportion to his creative potential. It is in this activity that the individual knows himself, for "you never find yourself until you face the truth" (Pearl Bailey).

Even though we are a synthesis of the universe, and we can therefore understand, in our limited reality, the laws of this same universe, through our interaction with it, in speaking of the universe, we are only referring to known material reality, not the many alien universes that remain unknown to the vast majority.

These alien planets and existences are offered only to those who can remember them, and a human being must be extremely evolved to achieve such power. And yet, it is only when these visions are manifested that one can say that he is a prophet. For before that, other states, such as Buddhahood, arise, which, although necessary, are far and far below spiritual perfection, which begins only with the exclusion of the context of humanity, an exclusion which includes all the universes of life existing in many galaxies.

This is why we can affirm that life is infinite. From the measure of our knowledge and awareness, there is infinity. But we can also say that life is finite and changeable if we attend to its permanent transformation in the physical realm.

In an exemplary way, it is as important to control the rotation of a planet as the temperature of a stove, since in the material universe all matter obeys the same laws except that which has been transformed to fit a universe that has distinguished itself within the divine law. And yet we can say that he who cannot control a planet has not yet reached the highest possible state, as much as the one who burns himself while cooking is losing himself. It is not by chance that unhappiness and widespread depression are behind the vast majority of accidents.

The vast majority of human beings live in such a dormant state that they cannot realize that what they consider to be normal is far below an ideal human level. And therefore they ignore the possibility of controlling a planet. But this possibility is always accessible to all who dreamed high enough to change the planet, whether with new forms of transport, beliefs, policies, transactions or technologies.

One day will come, when the power of a human being transcends his financial ambition or altruism for humanity, to become a consciousness that, through empathy, conquers the hearts of all. Until that day, financial ambition will continue to be the most favorable medium for a spiritual ascent, for no one will ever be truly rich without understanding the dynamics of abundance, and the dynamics of extreme poverty. For in the elements that distinguish both, we find everything we need, such as: Knowledge; Faith; Imagination; Determinism; Persistence; Inspiration; Cooperation; Ambition.

What is the Relationship Between Human Beings?

Considering that the Divine law is largely unknown, we can only, through the material universe of planet earth, know the norms by which they govern, in order to understand the order that arises from the chaos of our existences. But we can not assume that the material laws of this planet are similar to those of other planets, especially in other galaxies. In every reality on every planet where there is life, every being in such world controls the energy that moves matter in proportion to his potential. Thus, we can say that human potential is proportional to the state of the planet, physical and historical, in which he is. We are both a product of our ambitions and motivations, and the result of the ambitions and motivations of others. Some, extremely motivated, read the books that others, also motivated, wrote. Others ignore everything, whether it is their need to learn, or to pass on the knowledge they have acquired.

Very few people on this planet are determined on the path to getting mental resources to improve their lives. In fact, most are so focused on financial resources, or the means of obtaining them, namely a car and a good job, that they completely forget and ignore their potential as human beings. Only in moments of the life of some people, especially moments of great tribulation, some stop to think about this source of resources, constantly present in the life of all. We could even say that the polarity of planet earth, certifies that never an extreme is as catastrophic as its opposite. And so it is so interesting to see that billions of people are as stupid as an unproductive pig, and on the other hand, there have never been so many books in all of history, including books so many people can acquire free of charge. For the first time in history, thousands of books written over 100 years ago have become public domain, reflecting the history of consciousness for more than fifteen thousand years.

The same can be said about loneliness, a growing phenomenon in a world that has also proportionally increased its population by more than 6 billions in just a few decades.

In this sense, all the impossibilities that life manifests reflect the opposite polarity, because the differences are as obvious as the capacity to change reality is simple. That is, there have never been so many poor people on the planet, and yet, banks have never lent so much money as now.

The improbability of something has never been so present in the minds of so many people, who nevertheless share the same space. And yet, it is always interesting for me to see how those who complain about their problems always draw me into their lives, and reject responses through insults to my work. It's interesting to write books like this in coffee shops, while listening to people by my side, describing problems for which this and other books I've written offer answers. It is interesting to lose motivation to write in my apartment, and to feel that motivation and concentration increase whenever I am in public, because without this motivation I could not write so many books so fast, a motivation that comes from the energy of others, their thoughts, despite the fact that when I introduce myself and say what I do, they reject me as if I were a dangerous madman.

I even venture to say that the differences between humans are as relevant as their similarities are interesting. And even more interesting is when two completely different people fall in love, because the person who spends a lifetime suffering, finds me, awakens in me this love, and then destroys everything with insults. And all this time, she was unable to read and understand the books I offered for free, making me feel worthless. A feeling that certainly finds its opposite when I receive messages and emails from Singapore, the United States, Australia, and many other countries around the world, thanking me for my work and effort in improving their lives.

Love that does not find reciprocity in the reality in which it manifests itself, is often felt through a non-manifesting reality. And in this sense, the dream and reality are just the opposite of each other.

Can We Really Learn From Experience?

If we can understand the essence that makes a problem a dilemma, we can more easily avoid getting it in the future. And so, in the school of life, we learn to create happiness considering that a problem is only that in the absence of a solution. By learning about problems, we also learn about solutions, their best ways and strategies, and, in essence, about the purpose of our existence. He who knows how to do his work from home and knows is dynamic in learning from life, through the study that reality allows him to assimilate, can achieve good results in this school and live the peace and joy of a life full of successful accomplishments. This, however, is not possible without action in the direction of knowledge accumulated through the experience of other human beings like us who have experienced and lived the same.

Many people now call themselves 'students of the University of Life' as if experience theorized in the lack of knowledge led to some wisdom or even less, such as the ability to think and process information outside the models of personal validation. It is very easy to explain what you see, it is what humanity has done throughout history, but true education ends in the last book you read and can be evaluated by the amount of books you have read, understood and appreciated. Less than this, only allows us to be certified in stupidity. And this is what the "students of life" really are: fragile egos trying to justify their stupidity with arrogance, crystallizing their state of ignorance in time with pride. For although humanity has become confused with mechanics itself, there remains the transitory fact that knowledge, in any form or form, arises from books. And over 99% of all books ever produced in the history of mankind are now, thanks to the internet, freely available, in the public domain, and wherever a computer and electricity are present.

This truth also contributes extensively to the fact that humans are now, for the first time, choosing to deliberately remain ignorant. And this is what the "students of life" really are: proud manifestos of ignorance. They do not know that if you read enough to be smart, you will be too smart to explain what you are reading and too busy to share it.

So what can we say about those who become obsessed with their physical appearance whenever they have time for something? The premise is self-explanatory: the only real student is the "student of the self."

What is Reality?

The reality in which we exist is made up of innumerable illusory elements which, led by an energy composition, assume a purpose in correlation with our spiritual needs. The terrestrial reality, therefore, solidifies a set of lines of communication, in which nothing is exactly real but everything is necessary. In other words, "the greatest truth can not be put into words" (Lao Tzu). This is because it is interdynamic, and it does not exist without determinism, action and belief.

Material reality is transformed and our consciousness develops with it, so the function of reality is to aid the development of consciousness. With the development of consciousness, it will become equitably reality. Therefore, all technological development always appears on an equal plane to the capacity of the human being to use it.

We can say that between the energy that unites the various material bodies, including ours, and the association of our consciousness with all this process, there are lines of communication, before which we must understand the designs of our existence through the knowledge of reality itself. It implies, in the material reality, what we can understand in it, and it makes sense in our existence what, in the same reality, allows us to interact, creating lines of communication that feed a constant flow of self-understanding through action on this same reality. Thus we can affirm that the purpose of reality is to aid the development of understanding through knowledge of the cause-and-effect laws governing such reality. As our understanding develops, the reality that surrounds us will change.

In a broader sense, we can affirm that reality assumes the characteristics necessary for our present spiritual state, so that it will become a function of it and a direct association with it, even if the material universe has a speed of transformation itself.

Although there are no abrupt and spontaneous transformations, there are slow transformative speeds, and also so many so fast that they escape the perception of the mind. Between the two states, the slowest is at the level of the mind, the fastest at the level of consciousness, and the most extraordinary at the level of the subconscious.

The mind is composed of beliefs, consciousness is based on empirical knowledge, and the extraordinary lies in the field of faith, emotions and imagination. Reality is simply the result of the equation composed by the elements mentioned. And yet, it is extremely easy to predict the future of any individual simply by looking at what this individual believes.

Beliefs are really something very powerful because if you believe you can be rich without reading a book, or learning through someone successful, and are not able to change that belief through your experiences, you will probably fail at your goals.

The great billionaires who created all the wealth on their own, not only had big dreams, but also an equal capacity to be transformed. And this polarity was what really allowed them to get what they wanted.

In general, it may seem psychopathic, the habit of having inner conversations, with our imaginary self of the idealized future, dreaming of something that does not match the real, and even abdicating the personality and ego, systematically altering the concept of "I" for our purposes, but it is also a very spiritual process. Real psychopaths cannot do the same. The mechanics are very similar, but a psychopath is more focused on controlling others to achieve his ends, than changing behavior. And any individual who wants to get rich knows that honesty and cooperation are the fastest way to achieve it.

A lie never goes very far. In this sense, it is hardly possible for a psychopath to enrich himself, unless he obtains a social position that allows him to do so. It is not by chance that the greatest psychopaths choose politics as the ideal plan for it. It is the only profession that allows you to achieve enormous power without having to justify it by practice and with results. Any idiot with the ability to persuade by word, can win political elections.

One day, when I was a teenager, my idiot, biological father, showed me his irritation at dinner, when he heard reporters say that through an investigation they discovered that the prime minister did not really have any college degree.

People get scandalized with very little. But I interrupted his irritation to tell him: "A politician does not need a college degree. Anyone can be a politician." And at this moment, I could read his thoughts in full. The first thought, of course, was: "Can I be president of the republic?"; and the thought that followed was, "but no one will ever vote for me because I'm an idiot and I do not know what to say or what to do."

Life boils down to this, to this example mentioned above, which can be summed up in consciousness of ignorance. And that does not come without empirical knowledge about reality.

What is the Purpose of Life?

Given the fact that a human being aims to learn to know himself and to know his spiritual manifestation through life experiences, the meaning of it is summed up in the development of spiritual awareness. This awareness is recognized on the principle that a person will be rooting correctly whenever he feels happiness. Therefore, in unhappiness, you will know the meaning of being wrong in this walk. In this sense, everything that produces lasting happiness, belongs to the spiritual purposes of the individual.

It can be said that, although material objects can produce happiness, it is a happiness of short duration, because the objects themselves, and the material reality as a whole, are not the reason for our happiness, but only the vehicle to reach it. Many people, with a very limited ability to understand reality, believe they will be happy when they can get a luxury car and a mansion. They forget that these are consequences of long-term plans, which they will never be able to ensure, because they do not have persistence, do not know how to suffer in the long run for an immaterial purpose.

In fact, people would more easily achieve their goals if they started out wanting something they really need or if they were focused on the path to the goal rather than the desire to achieve something. That is, if they learned to like what they do, and decided to do something they like, not just what allows them to attract wealth. That is why it is said that "the truth will set you free but first it will make you miserable" (Jim Davis).

If we look at the acquisition of money, for example, it is relatively obvious that it is the services and objects necessary to the public that attract wealth, not the exaggerated desire to be rich without offering any benefit in return to society.

If we allow ourselves to be attached to the materiality that gives shape to illusions, we will experience unhappiness. Because, whenever we acquire the material good for which we have fought, we will feel that this object does not fill us. In this feeling of emptiness, we will successively look for new objects, living a growing emptiness and permanent unhappiness. Even before reaching these goals, we forget them, whenever life gives us a little pleasure.

People who find a job offering food, and get enough money to travel three times a year, easily forget their wealth ambitions, mainly because they imply a much worse lifestyle than the previous one.

One of my companions was very supportive when I told her that I was going to give up my job as a university professor and the huge and very comfortable apartment we lived in, as well as the many trips we took each year. Then, once she began to experience the new reality, became bitter, toxic, insulting, and very aggressive and resentful. For now we were living in a rented room, we were no longer traveling, and I always saved as much as possible on all expenses. We argued much more than before, until I broke up, abandoning her. And that's when I got rich. I still had to spend a few more months working hard to get that result, but in six months I was rich. Then I traveled a lot, for six months, but alone. She, on the other hand, found a rich man who could not go anywhere, because he had a job as a lawyer that would not let him. Her life had become an unpleasant monotony. And I started a relationship later with a much more attractive person and within my expectations, after realizing that my ability to attract the opposite sex had increased substantially. For, as soon as I became single, I not only worked much more in my business, but also got more free time to do sport and lose weight.

The spirit cannot be filled with illusions, so the right path will naturally have to be another. The path of spiritual discovery that feeds the spirit resides in soul consciousness for its most elemental right to find happiness. But this path can, to a large extent, be composed of unhappiness. On the other hand, are we really unhappy when we do something that gives us happiness? When we have a companion, or friend, who supports us, when we work daily from morning until night to achieve one goal, everything else becomes secondary, and possibilities and opportunities become more visible. It is as if our faith attracted miracles. And if we have to assign a role to love, that would be the best way to explain love and compassion in a couple. There is only true love in sharing dreams. And if we want to speak in self-love, in this particular case, it is only present when our actions correspond to our dreams.

For each being, this right will find different parameters that have answers at the heart of the individual personality. And it is in self-learning and searching what allows us to live with greater happiness, that we find a harmony between the consciousness and the mind that thinks about the real world. What makes us dream, what warms us and calms the heart, is the gateway to our spiritual path.

What is the Relationship Between Our Desires and Spirituality?

It is quite natural that in the early stages of spiritual evolution, dreams are presented as very material, and only then become less material and more and more emotional.

We are primarily connected to our most basic needs, whether they are related to survival, sex, or the desire to belong to something, a group, a nation, a purpose that connects us to the world. In a first phase, the dream can lead the way of owning a home, where we can feel at peace and harmony with ourselves. It may even be related to living in a certain country, under certain socioeconomic conditions. In a second phase, we can dream about what can contribute to that peace and harmony, just like someone to keep us company and help us to become a better person. In a third phase, we will desire only peace and harmony, seeking to attract everything and everyone who can contribute to it. This state, striking because it is more connected with our emotions, is easier to attain.

In the path of happiness we find our purpose. And because the purpose of each being is different, the paths to happiness may cross and even be in some cases parallel, but they will always be unique. The learning we get from those we meet along the way helps us to become a better person. In a couple, for example, each one of the partners walks alone, but the paths of both reside in the existential joint harmony, reason why the unique learnings they must realize are in this same existence in love. And often one's dissatisfaction contributes to the reinforcement of the relationship, such as when a woman does not like her job and her boyfriend, businessman, is coincidentally looking for an assistant, or when a person has problems for which the person in his or her life has the answers. It is for this reason that love exists to unite people who must learn together. This does not mean, however, that we have a duty to help others, because to know love is also to know how to accept love, and unfortunately not everyone wants to be helped.

In love, we find greater complementarity between what we can do for the other and what we need them to do for us, but self-determination for good and for evil continues to exist. Still, we find here the support we need when we no longer have the strength to go alone. And, therefore, love is indispensable to all those who have lost the strength to continue giving meaning to their lives.

The most unhappy people are those who lack love the most and it is really hard to love ourselves. The human being was not designed to live in solitude. This work, although possible, is very hard. In love, life gains more color and purpose, so love increases the need to live and facilitates that pleasure, when both are mature enough to recognize their differences, similarities, needs and complementarity. When we love, we are concerned with the other, with their needs, and we are in tune with existence. For this reason, love is one of the greatest and most important drivers of the meaning of life.

For many people, loving represents the only time they experience responsibility or empathy at a deeper level. And although this is true for love relationships, we can also say that it is valid for everything else, because the meaning of life is also the way of self-love, even if we need the sense of belonging to understand self-love. In many cases it is separation, divorce, loneliness, which awakens in people the need for self-love, and forces them to learn to understand it, not only through a more satisfying existence, but also more respectful partners.

Why Does Love Exist?

In order to find a meaning for our existence we must learn to love ourselves. This kind of love is different from that which is expressed physically with a partner.

Of course, when we are loved, it is easier to like ourselves, and that is why we need the love of others. Such confidence can hardly be fabricated.

When we experience the love of others, we believe that our existence is helpful to them, and for this reason, we begin to love ourselves. It is a love based on mutual help and sharing of emotions. In other words, love only manifests itself when there is trust, honesty and interest in contributing to the happiness of another person. But these principles are also the basis of self-esteem, i.e., confidence in our ability to overcome difficulties, honesty in our goals and interest in contributing to our personal happiness through projects, plans and habits that promote it.

Do you think that a person who gets into the habit of drinking too much alcohol, smoking drugs or tobacco, and wasting her time with parties, and promiscuity is trying to be happy? No. This person is ignoring your need to be happy. She has given up on herself. And now she's just trying to live with this situation.

In self-love we get more will to live and, in the will to live, we will seek what makes us happy, maintaining the purpose of our experience. When we find this purpose, we no longer lack the love of the other, but we will maintain it, because now it is no longer a necessity, but a complement to the existential purpose that we have found. And that is why self-love also makes us aware of toxic and destructive relationships. In fact, the first thing a psychopath or narcissist does to his partners is to destroy his self-love, otherwise he could not control them and force them to satisfy selfish needs, to the detriment of their own.

On the other hand, he or those we truly love find meaning within that same dynamic. And so the sense of love can come in two forms: The love we need to love ourselves the most; The self-love that leads us to seek who complements it. In both cases, love never assumes human preconditions or rules.

Love is perfect in itself, and therefore, in one way or another, it always complements itself. For self-love leads in the direction of love of the other, and love of the other leads in the sense of self-love. Even when we love someone who does not know how to love us back, but only hurt, we can understand this. In the happiness of living, we find the meaning of love and, by giving it meaning, we find the purpose of our existence. With those we love, we understand more about who we are and our role in the world, and by understanding this, we can better understand what paths we must take to develop spiritually. We will find them in whatever we do, which increases our self-esteem and love for others. This is because, in this process, we will take actions that produce positive or negative results.

In this experience, we will become aware of the rules that make up existence. The more we know them, the better we will know how to act to produce more happiness and less misery, knowing that in happiness we get more pleasure in living.

Life is therefore a journey to understand the rules that govern it, for in its materiality we learn to live in this world, but in its infinite logic, we learn about ourselves, about life, about the universe and, ultimately, about the purpose of God.

How to Achieve Happiness?

Happiness can best be gained when we intensify the pleasure in existence because it is proportional to our attitude in life. In this sense, in the course of this journey, we learn to know ourselves by choosing or refusing to face what makes us feel good. In these decisions, we find greater pleasure in being, and through this pleasure we are attuned to our spiritual purpose.

The mistakes we make tend to be visible later when we look back at our decisions because people rarely realize that only decisions that have positive long-term effects can be taken as positive decisions. Obviously, we do not include here substances that cause any kind of addiction, whether physical or emotional.

In what makes us happy, we learn more about who we are and the reason for our existence, but only when the choices are constructive and in the sense of our spiritual liberation. As we walk along this path, we will transform and realize more about our real need for material scope, understanding the emotional implications of it. For in the end we find a connection between all decisions and the way each interconnects with the others.

Throughout our life, we will always and gradually make new choices, and in this way, we will, in a permanent correlation between transformations in the material plane and transformations of the personality, better know our unique purpose, thus becoming more and more happy. The only difficulties we will encounter in this process that can stop us are the need to separate ourselves from those who will not be able to assimilate our transformations and will often resist them, namely those whose existence is more interconnected with our. It is not by chance that the need to follow certain demanding paths, such as the creation of a business, often imply ending relationships that do not accept the demands that this entails.

Happiness is the search for the meaning of life, which is found in what gives us existential pleasure. "The love of truth has its reward in heaven and on earth" (Friedrich Nietzsche). To dream, to work to acquire our dreams, and to live daily in the sense of fulfilling dreams, allows for more pleasure and fits perfectly into existential purposes.

It is in the harmony between the dream and the reality that the being finds the way to his happiness. And obviously, as we find ourselves in a material reality, we have to live, modify and act on the objects that make up that reality, as well as the people who interact in it, in order to create a necessary link between reality and the dream. As an example, we must understand that the dream produces a positive energy that is associated with the energy that moves the material world, and in this association we attract what we dream, but it is in our decisions and actions that the dream materializes or not.

In this correlation, both dream and reality are transformed. And it would not be possible to be realistic in a dream, or motivated with faith in our reality, if we were not able to adjust both through the process of understanding ourselves by acting upon them. For life is, ultimately, a metacognitive system, in which we understand ourselves through the implications in our actions of trying to understand the world. No decision is lacking in implications.

Imagining that we are dreaming about obtaining something, if, whenever the reality brings us an opportunity to obtain it, we reject this opportunity, we will, over time, because we do not reach the dream, think that we will never be able to achieve it, and we will stop dreaming. But reality does not stop attracting what we want with our wrong decisions, but with our ceasing to dream.

The reality we see is also the one we believe to exist. And so, if we focus more on the physical world we will have more difficulty in dreaming. On the other hand, if we focus too much on dreams without paying attention to the opportunities of the physical world, we will hardly be able to take advantage of the opportunities provided to us. Both states are important because the more dreams we are able to realize, the more self-esteem we will have, and in that happiness we will find the self-confidence that allows us to continue to dream.

It is in the dream that life moves. Happiness lies in the intense dream accompanied by an intense life in the sense of reaching it. And a life with purpose is a happy life.

About the Publisher

This book was published by the 22 Lions Bookstore.
For more books like this visit www.22Lions.com.
Join us on social media at:
Fb.com/22Lions;
Twitter.com/22lionsbookshop;
Instagram.com/22lionsbookshop;
Pinterest.com/22LionsBookshop.

www.ingramcontent.com/pod-product-compliance
Lightning Source LLC
Chambersburg PA
CBHW050450010526
44118CB00013B/1771